KEYS TO DELIVERING AMAZING CUSTOMER SERVICE

by

Errol D. Allen

EAC Media P.O. Box 420081 Houston, Tx 77242

Library of Congress Cataloging-in-Publication Data

Allen, Errol
Keys to delivering amazing customer service
by Errol Allen

ISBN 978-1-300-08019-0

Acknowledgements

Special thanks go out first of all to my wife **Theresa** for her encouragement and support of my writing this book. To my friends **Jerry Phillips, Kenneth Frank, Donald Lawson, Carl Hill and Richard Polk** for walking with me along life's journey. Thanks also go out to my friend **Ken Marsh**, author of **Fearless Networking**, for feeling that my message was important enough for me to sit down and share with others. To my friend **Dan Valdez** for giving my first speaking engagement which gave me confidence that yes, someone understood my message. To leadership consultant **Linda Stiles** for her encouragement when I began this journey as a customer service consultant. To **Steve Levine**, publisher of **Small Business Today Magazine, Keith Davis Sr.**, publisher of **DMars Business Journal and Ian Miller,** publisher of **Customer Service Manager** for allowing me to be a contributing writer in their publications. To my friend **Hank Moore,** author of **The Business Tree**, for his wisdom and willingness to tell others about my passion for customer service. To my friend **Walter Blanchard** for his encouragement of my mission as a customer service consultant. To **Bonnie Karpay**, author of **Without Notice – Life Can Change In A Moment** for introducing me to some amazing people. To all of my **LinkedIn** article readers – thanks for your support and kind comments. Thanks to **William Spencer** of **Social Media Footprints,** for without his social media expertise I would not have any **LinkedIn** article readers!

Thanks to all of my former employers for the various opportunities and experiences – for it is from these various viewpoints that this book is written.

Contents

Preface – My Philosophy   I

Why A Customer Service Strategy?   IV

Chapter 1 – Establish Core Values – Who Are You?   1

Chapter 2 – Be Passionate About Your Business   7

Chapter 3 - Be the Expert   11

Chapter 4 - Carefully Select Your Customer Contact Employees and   15
    Train Them Well

Chapter 5 - Develop Fair Employee Reward Systems   24

Chapter 6 – Managing For Great Customer Service   29

Chapter 7 – Create Employee and Customer Friendly Processes   35

Chapter 8 - Leaders - Spend Time On The Front Line   40

Chapter 9 – Be Accessible & Responsive   47

Chapter 10 – Properly Assess Your Customer's Needs   63

Chapter 11 – Clarify Expectations and Meet/Exceed Them   66

Chapter 12 – Customize When Necessary   71

Chapter 13 – Communicate – Keep Your Customer Informed   75

Chapter 14 – Establish Relationships With Your Customers   79

Chapter 15 – Create A Thank You System   83

Chapter 16 – The Disgruntled Customer   87

Chapter 17 – Create A Customer Complaint System   91

Chapter 18 – Create A Customer Feedback System   97

Summary   103

My Philosophy

After spending 25+ years in the customer service industry, I have been exposed to both good and not so good customer service systems. There have been instances where the company spoke about the need to put the customer first yet had no idea or inclination to really understand what that means and how to do it. At other times, a need to focus on the customer was identified, a strategy developed and implemented, but when the process became difficult or certain management roles changed, interest waned and soon the plan became not so important. I have experienced systems where the customer service personnel did not receive proper product knowledge training yet were held accountable for properly servicing the customer. There were instances of non-communication between departments resulting in frustrating experiences for employees and customers.

One company did not take into consideration the customer service personnel workload when developing employee performance standards nor were employees allowed to voice their opinion regarding the imbalance without fear of reprisal. Yet this company could not understand why the employee frustration level was always high and performance results seemed stuck below the desired level. I have also been fortunate enough to have spent 9 years at a company that understood the necessity to train its customer contact personnel properly, sought and valued employee input, balanced rewards and workloads, and believed in leadership training. While not a perfect situation, this company saw the

I

benefit of its actions via low employee turnover, customer retention - even as competition increased – and long term profitability.

My customer service philosophy is based upon my experiences while in the day to day situations with a customer, both over the phone and face to face. It is also based upon my experiences as the manager of a customer service team. My philosophy reflects time spent as an operations analyst, responsible for analyzing various operations to identify opportunities for greater efficiencies. It's based upon time spent creating performance standards for properly delivering a fair performance review. The experience of creating a training program for front line employees is included in my customer service philosophy.

I lean toward describing my customer service philosophy as one based upon a systemic mindset. Systemic in the belief that great customer service is a product of multiple components. A great customer service system should contain not only friendly, service oriented personnel, but customer and employee friendly processes. Employees should feel valued just as a company expects the employee to value the customer. Performance goals must take into consideration the workloads the employee encounters on a regular basis. Fear must be driven out of the work environment in order for fresh ideas to be heard and implemented. Customer opinions should be solicited on a regular basis to identify opportunities for improving the customer experience. Management must establish core values describing how everyone will interact with each other and with the customers.

This may all appear to be too time-consuming to develop and implement. It is worth all of the time and effort required as a company's long term success is at stake. The unwillingness to create a customer service system limits a company in their ability to attain the highest possible level of success. This is true for the small business owner as well as large corporations. While progress may seem slow at first when attempting to change the cultural mindset at an existing company, it is imperative for long term survival. A start-up has the perfect opportunity to create from scratch a balanced systemic environment resulting in the creation of loyal customers and loyal employees. In either case, it is my opinion that all the necessary effort should be made in order to create a great customer service system. Let's begin down the road of creating a balanced customer service system.

Why Develop A Customer Service Strategy?

In the quest to become successful in business, it's important to develop a strategy. To most business owners, this means creating a business plan, creating a support team – attorney, accountant, etc. I propose that an additional strategy receive the same priority – your customer service strategy. You might say, 'Why is it important for me to develop a customer service strategy?" Let me give you a few reasons.

Sixty-eight percent of customer defections take place because customers feel poorly treated. Ninety-six percent of these defecting customers do so without bothering to say why they've chosen to utilize a competitor. Would you agree that it's important that your customers don't feel poorly treated? Is it not important to make sure that they consistently receive the highest level of service? Let's consider another reason. How much does it cost to obtain a new customer and how does that compare to the cost of retaining an existing customer. For a small business owner, the cost to obtain a customer on average is $250.00 while the cost to retain an existing customer is said to be substantially less than that at ten to twenty percent of the cost to obtain a new customer. Imagine the cost to obtain a new customer for a midsize to large company! Even more of a reason to develop a customer service strategy. Let's go on to another reason.

A 5% reduction in the customer defection rate can increase profits by 25% to 125% depending upon the industry. Let's try another method to explain. Customer service is what drives the success of any business. Some would surely say 'No Errol, a great product or service concept drives the success on any business." While that statement is somewhat true, a great product or service concept without great customer service is like expecting your beautiful garden flowers to flourish without your giving attention to them. I have often found that you don't get upper management's or the business owner's full attention regarding customer service unless you provide the financial impact of customer service to the company.

Customer service has a dual role as it both creates and preserves revenue. Let me explain while I believe this to be true. Customer service creates revenue via the word of mouth avenue. When a great product or service is coupled with great customer service, your customers become your ambassadors. Their willingness to speak positively about your business leads to additional customers, thereby creating additional revenue. Recent research by the **Technical Assistance Research Program (TARP)** indicates that for every ten people hearing either positive or negative "word of mouth" information, one person takes action. That one new customer, should they receive the level of service expected, will in turn keep the positive "word of mouth" cycle in motion. Another form of revenue creation as a result of great customer service is price increases. **TARP** has also studied the impact of price increases on the customer's willingness to do business with companies. In a study of the banking industry, only 10% of survey respondents who had not experienced a customer service related problem expressed dissatisfaction with an increase in fees and charges. This means that 90% of survey respondents were okay with the price increases due to the level of customer service provided by their particular bank.

In regards to customer service acting as a revenue preserver, there is one question that must be answered before we continue: How much is your customer worth to your business? Whether your company is small or large, the need to determine what your customer is worth to your business is critical when calculating the amount of revenue being preserved and produced by addressing customer service related issues. For example, let's say that your business has 1,000 customers and the average annual revenue generated by each customer is $400.00. If 10% of those customers experience service related problems, that's 100 customers. Bear with me as we start the calculations. Now let's assume that 50% of those customers don't even bother to complain, they just simply go away. Their decision to leave without complaining represents $20,000.00 in lost revenue. What about the other 50% that do complain? Let's say that you're able to satisfy 40% (20), 40% (20) become frustrated with your attempts to satisfy and 20% (10) remain dissatisfied. So now let's consider the repurchase behavior of those complaining customers. Should 10% (2) of the customers that you're able to satisfy after they complain decide to not repurchase, that represents $800.00 in lost revenue. In the frustrated with your attempts to satisfy group, 25 % (5) discontinue purchases with your company, which represents $2000.00 in revenue. On to the customers that remain dissatisfied after complaining - 60% (6) of this group decide not to repurchase from your company, which means an additional $2400.00 in lost revenue. The total potential annual revenue lost in this scenario is $25,200.00! Wait, there's more. Remember the "word of mouth" factor discussed earlier. These dissatisfied customers will tell others about their experience with your company. In this scenario, when you consider the 50 customers that left without complaining, add the 13 customers that complained yet decided not to repurchase, that's 63 customers who have the potential to utilize negative "word of mouth" marketing. If these dissatisfied customers tell 10 additional people about their experiences (630 people) and 1 in 10 acts on the information (63 people), there's potential revenue missed due to dissatisfied customers. Even if the new customers' average annual purchases equal $300.00, you're still possibly facing $18900.00 in lost potential revenue. Don't forget about the cost side of poor customer service - the employee costs to resolve customer complaints and the material costs when rework is required to satisfy the customer. Take this example and apply your real numbers to determine the financial impact to your business. Whew! Lots of calculations, but it's definitely worth it when it comes to determining the financial impact of customer service. The key to preserving revenue is to:

1. Be consistent in your service delivery and **2. Encourage your customers to complain.** Consistency in your service delivery leads to loyalty, less complaints and even more important, fewer reasons for the silent defections of the non-complainers. Encourage your customers to complain as this gives you an opportunity to retain their business. The example above illustrates the financial impact of non-complaining customers. Offer multiple ways to complain - at the point of purchase, on your website, via chat, 1-800 #s. Don't forget to monitor social media for comments regarding your company and respond to the complaints in a timely manner. Remember; don't take customer service for granted. The financial impact is huge!!

Where Do We Begin

As we get started in identifying the keys to delivering amazing customer service, let me say that I'm a big advocate of beginning the process on the inside of your business first. This means taking a look at the framework of your establishment - whether yours is a small or large business. It means developing a set of guiding principles in regards to internal and external interactions. It means taking the time to acquire a level of knowledge about your product or service that incents your customer to trust your advice. It means understanding why passion for your business is important to the level of service received by the customer. It means examining your hiring procedures, employee training and managing methods. In my opinion, this is paramount to delivering great customer service. I hear someone asking "Why is this so Errol." I just believe that what's on the inside eventually makes itself apparent on the outside. That "outside" is where your purchasing customer lives. If you want to consistently deliver great customer service for your purchasing customer, it's important that the internal foundation is built and maintained with that goal in mind. Okay, now let's proceed on this road of developing amazing customer service!

Chapter 1- Establish Core Values

During my stint as an operations analyst at one particular corporation, it became apparent that all was not equal at this company. If an employee knew certain members of management, they were allowed certain "privileges". The level of service provided to customers seemed secondary to what certain employees felt they were entitled. While having a conversation with a call center manager at the operations desk, the desk phone rang which I promptly answered. "I would like to speak with Margie" was the request on the other end of the line. I advised this person that Margie was taking inbound calls, but if you provide me with your name and number, I will have Margie call you on her next break. "Who is this?" was her reply. After identifying myself, she abruptly ended the call. Within ten minutes, my manager's manager was at my desk asking to have a word with me. He leaned over saying "I just got a call from Margie regarding your conversation. Just keep doing what you're doing to help get this place in order." While I was happy to have his blessing, it was apparent that this person was comfortable in attempting to get the ear of someone that she felt was a "friend in high places" to get her way. I could imagine her saying, "Who does this new guy think he is?" I could see that some basic principles were absent at this company. Did core values regarding employee interaction and customer service even exist at this place?

1

The establishment of core values for your business creates a framework from which you will make daily decisions. Core values help to establish the identity of the company – what you stand for and why you do things the way you do. When core values are created, the principles of the company's existence spring forth. Everyone within the company must adhere to these principles. Rank must not be a reason for someone to be allowed to act in a manner not representative of the core values. Leaders within the organization must set the example if others are expected to take the core values seriously. In regards to providing great customer service, a good set of core values should include the following: 1. How we will treat each other within the company. 2. How we will treat our customers. Here are four principles I suggest using when developing core values.

Principle of Respect - Every person by the fact that they are a human being deserves a measure of respect. In my opinion, the same holds true regarding customers. Every customer deserves a measure of respect, even when their actions are somewhat callous and uncaring; it's still possible to show basic respect during these encounters. It's been my experience that when one remains respectful during customer interactions, there's usually a positive outcome to the interaction. How many of you have received a call back or return visit from a customer who was blatantly disrespectful to apologize for their actions? This would not be possible without a conscious decision to always give every customer a measure of respect. On another note, some companies give priority based upon customer size or revenue. While it's smart to know how much a customer contributes to the bottom line, be careful not to make your smaller customer feel unimportant. Treat all customers with respect – make sure they know how important they are to your organization's success. Employees should treat each other with respect across the organization. One's position or status does not exempt one from this principle. Internal respect becomes respect shown to the customer. Make sure this principle is very apparent within your organization as the failure to do so will most certainly impact customer service.

Principle of Service - It seems to me that the main goal of any organization providing a product or service is to be of service to those that call, visit – in person or via web or are visited by a representative of that organization. Service is defined as "an act of helpful activity; help; aid". How can those of us in the customer service industry be more helpful to those that we serve? Can we take the time to really help our customers or are we more concerned with being measured while helping the customer? Are our actions really "helpful activities" or are we providing just enough help to satisfy the customer for the short-term because our metric says it's time to end the interaction? Customers expect to be serviced in a timely manner, with a certain measure of respect by someone who is interested in doing what's best for the customer. Organization leaders are responsible for developing a culture whose main purpose is to properly service the customer.

Principle of Integrity – I think that I'm safe in saying that most organizations seek to operate with a high level of integrity. Integrity is defined as "adherence to moral and ethical principles; soundness of moral character; honesty." This principle requires an organization to ask itself "Are we doing what's right for our customers." "If we follow through with this decision, what will the impact be to our customers?" "If we chose to ignore what we know about this situation, what is the long-term impact to our company's reputation with our customers? This principle requires one to be above-board at all times with customers. It is imperative that customers feel that they can trust your organization. Today's customer can create a whirlwind of negativity via the social media channel. Numerous examples exist where an organization was not forthcoming with information that impacted the customer – in some cases the situation was life threatening! Once again, leaders are responsible for setting the tone here.

Principle of Pride in Workmanship - One's satisfaction in providing the best possible service to a customer is a form of pride in workmanship. It's no secret that a lot of front line people feel they're unable to provide the best experience due to time constraints imposed by organizational metrics. It's important to be able to go the extra mile in servicing the customer without the fear of negative repercussions. This principle in action creates both customer and employee satisfaction. Customers benefit greatly when employees take the time to do what's necessary to provide a customer service experience that fully satisfies their reason for contacting the company. Most employees feel good about their ability to utilize their skills to fully meet a customer's needs, especially when it involves resolving an issue that could mean the difference between losing or retaining a customer. When given the proper time to service a customer, it's my belief that most employees will do what's necessary to make sure the customer is satisfied at the end of the interaction. Most people like to feel good about the level of service they provide – it's just something about knowing that your actions resulted in a positive outcome for another person. Set your metrics to afford your service providers enough time to properly service the customer. If it's possible, measure how many of your customer interactions are the result of their not being serviced properly the first time.

In order for great customer service to flow out to the customer, greatness must be the goal on the inside of the business. How can you accomplish this you ask? Words such as honesty, respect, integrity and attitude must be incorporated into the core values of your business. Indoctrinate the core values throughout your organization. When hiring new employees, make sure that your core values are fully understood before the person begins day to day duties. Incorporate your core values into your performance standards. Great companies such as **Zappos**, **Southwest Airlines** and **The Dwyer Group** all operate from a good set of core values. Visit their websites to get ideas for developing core values for your business. Businesses of all sizes, from the one man operation to the multinational corporation, should have core values.

Exercise

1. Develop a list of words that identify your core values. Ex: **Respectful, Responsible, Integrity, etc.**

2. Use your list of words to develop core value sentences. Ex: **We will exhibit respect at all times to each other within the company and to our customers.**

3. Examine your performance standards for evidence of your core values. Ex: **Associate is respectful of both fellow associates and customers.**

Chapter 2 - Be Passionate About Your Business

While attending a hospitality association meeting, the speaker talked about an encounter with a hotel desk clerk. He mentioned that the check in process was slow, but what seemed to irritate him most was the failure of the clerk to make eye contact and the clerk's nonchalant demeanor. According to the speaker, she seemed to lack passion for her job duties. What the clerk didn't know was this speaker is the owner of a chain of hotels!

Have you ever listened to someone that's excited about what they do or a recent positive experience? You can see and feel the emotion from this person! You're drawn closer to this person by their energy! The same should be said of you when you talk about your business or when servicing customers. Your customers or prospective customers must be able to see how passionate you are about your product/service. The energy that you exhibit transfers to your customers. Passion helps to sell your product/service. If you don't feel good about what you're offering, why should your customer? Your energy entices your customer to listen to what you're saying regarding your product/service. Watch your body language, voice cadence and walking speed. I know we all have been serviced by someone who appeared unconcerned, lacked enthusiasm or was slow of foot. How did this make you feel? I usually won't return for another round of this treatment. Make sure that your customer can see or hear your passion! Enthusiasm is contagious.

During a visit to a local clothing retailer to take advantage of an awesome sale, I was the recipient of a great example of passion and enthusiasm. After being greeted (right away!) and asked my reason for visiting the store, the sales clerk proceeded to offer his assistance in a most professional manner. After choosing two pairs of slacks, I asked him to guide me to the shirts that were on sale. He asked for my neck size and sleeve length, then measured both just to make sure. While looking through the shirts, I found a particular shirt that I considered a "must have" except there was one obstacle - the neck size was too small. The sales clerk turned up his service a notch at this point. He checked every shirt on the shelf that matched the one of interest, pulled out two of the largest boxes if I have ever seen in a clothing store from beneath a display table in search of that shirt! He then asked if I would allow him time to check in the back for the shirt. Unfortunately, the shirt was not in stock, but the sales clerk said "I can order it for you Mr. Allen and it will be here within three to five days." After all of his efforts, I couldn't turn him down. His passion and enthusiasm earned the sale for him!

There are three grocery stores (all owned by the same company) that I visit, with two of the three located a greater distance from my home that the third. Guess which store my wife and I most frequently utilize? Believe it or not, the two stores that are the furthest from our home. I hear you asking "Why is that Errol?" The store closest to our home is like entering a cave. The employees don't exhibit a lot of enthusiasm when interacting with the customers. They barely make eye contact! Now there could be multiple reasons for this, but we're just not comfortable shopping at this particular store. The two other stores are just the opposite. The employees are very enthusiastic and proactive in engaging with customers. We are willing to drive a greater distance to receive the better customer experience. Passion for your product or service is critical to your quest to provide great customer service. Make sure your business has a daily outbreak of passionomia and enthusiaminitis!

Exercise

1. Check your enthusiasm level before interacting with your customer. Practice speaking clearly, making eye contact and exhibiting energy regarding your product or service.

2. Gauge the enthusiasm level of your front line personnel by spending time in areas where your customer is being serviced. How's their voice tone? Body language okay?

3. Where appropriate, seek feedback from front line managers regarding the enthusiasm level of front line employees. Are there any unacknowledged issues that may be creating a negative environment?

Chapter 3 Be The Expert

One of my good friends here in Houston is well versed in social media. He recommended that I change my social media focus to LinkedIn in order to increase my brand awareness and to attract potential clients. Prior to his advice, I had feebly attempted to use other social media avenues to accomplish this, but was not really receiving a sufficient amount of traffic to my website. Because he is deemed an expert in social media, I took his advice. Within thirty days, people were aware of my blog articles and reading my online newsletter around the world! Guess whose social media advice I will trust and implement?

We've all spent time around someone that we felt was an expert in their particular field. Perhaps it was your dentist or doctor. Maybe it was the salesperson at the department store or even the mechanic who performs your automobile maintenance. How about that friend who seems to know everything there is to know about today's computer technology? Do you find yourself having the tendency to rely on the information or recommendations provided by these experts? Don't you know that you must consider yourself as the expert in your business if you want to retain customers? I'll explain why that's important.

11

When your customer contacts you regarding your products/services, they expect you to have the answers to their questions or solutions to their issues. If they feel that you are unable to provide either of these, they will seek assistance from one of your competitors. Ask yourself, if you required the assistance of a particular business, but did not get the impression that they were capable of meeting your needs, what would you do? I think we both know the answer.

A key factor in being an expert is the ability to ask the right questions. Before recommending usage of LinkedIn, my social media expert asked several questions – Who is your target market? What are you trying to communicate? How will you communicate your message? Your knowledge of your particular industry and of your products/services helps you to formulate the proper questions in your attempt to meet the need of your customers. This knowledge is gained through establishing the discipline to acquire knowledge about your industry and obtain a thorough understanding of your products/services. What are the trends in your industry? What ingredients/materials are included in your products? How does your product operate? What are the specifics about each service that you provide? How do your products/services compare to your competitors? How will your customer benefit by choosing you over your competitor? Your knowledge of each of these allows you to formulate questions that assist in developing the right solution for your customer's needs, wants or issues.

Early in my customer service career, I worked for a major corporation in the security systems industry. In my position on the evening shift, I often received inbound calls from business owners experiencing problems when attempting to set the alarm at the end of the day. My first few attempts at assisting did not go as smoothly as I would have liked, as I didn't possess an expert level of knowledge regarding the operation of the various alarm systems. Through gathering and studying the system operations manuals, my troubleshooting skill level increased until I felt and was treated like an expert regarding the operation of the various systems. I kept my trusty manuals handy until the information became ingrained in my brain. It felt good to be able to ask the right questions while assisting the customers with their alarm issues. The ability to do so helped me to formulate the proper solution to resolve the system problem. This was impossible without my acquiring the product knowledge.

Another byproduct of becoming an expert is that you build trust with your customer. When your customer is confident that you are indeed an expert, their trust level rises as they become comfortable within themselves that yes, you are in fact knowledgeable about your products/services. Once you obtain your customer's trust, a relationship (hopefully it's long term) begins. After a relationship develops, referrals are sure to follow. These referrals add to the long-term success of your business. Not only do you retain your present customers by becoming an expert, but you gain new customers via referrals because your customer deems you the expert!

Exercise

1. Identify the changes that have taken place within your industry over the last 5 years.

2. Identify the differences in yours and your competitors' products and services.

3. Identify the features of your products and services.

4. Spend time utilizing your products and services to get your customer's perspective.

Chapter 4 - Carefully Select Your Customer Contact Employees

A real good friend of mine from the Dallas, Texas area called to advise me of a great customer service experience. It seems that he was in need of a kitchen faucet and decided to visit the local big box hardware store. My friend was greeted by the department clerk and asked if he was in need of assistance. After explaining his reason for visiting, the clerk escorted my friend to kitchen faucets and provided assistance in choosing the best value vs the most expensive faucet. My friend also had additional questions regarding some fittings. Although the clerk was unfamiliar with the fittings, he requested assistance from another clerk who was successful in fulfilling the fitting request. The clerk then escorted my friend to the checkout area. Before leaving the store, my friend requested an opportunity to speak with the store manager in order to advise him of the great customer experience.

In previous chapters, we discussed the importance of being passionate about your business and why it's necessary to become an expert. If you have employees, it's important that they also possess those traits. Before we talk about how to make sure you hire the right employees, let's deal with why it's important. Are you serious about the service your customer receives? Remember, 68% of customers discontinue their relationship with a business because they feel poorly treated. What does this statistic indicate? It states that people within companies are treating the customer poorly. It's important to utilize good judgment when hiring customer contact personnel as your customer expects and deserves a certain level of customer service. Having managed customer service personnel, I know the positive impact of properly selecting who gets to service the customer.

The financial impact alone is a good reason to be selective. For example, let's say that as a result of not thoroughly qualifying a prospect you lose one customer. If that customer is worth $150.00 a month, then you lose $1800.00 annually. Now just for this discussion's sake, the employee costs you one customer per month over a one year period – now that's 12 lost customers. If these 12 customers all spend an average of $150.00 monthly, the total lost revenue is now $21,600.00. Seen enough? Don't forget the cost of training, salary and benefits that you've invested in the employee. Should you determine that this employee is no longer a good fit; your investment is lost as well. Oh yeah – don't forget that these lost customers talk to other potential customers, so now you've lost that potential revenue as well! How can you prevent this scenario from becoming a reality? I'll give you a few hiring tips:

1. **Hire Attitude** – While it's most common to hire experience, I believe that attitude should be top priority. Customer service requires one to have a mind-set of service.

2. This mind-set brings with it a belief for the need to always be ready to serve, to go the extra mile to make someone else happy. Remember, you can teach skills, but you can't teach attitude! When interviewing prospects, make inquiries regarding what gives the prospect the feeling of fulfillment at the end of the workday or in life in general. Listen for references along the lines of helping, serving or resolving issues.

3. **Hire Energy** – Having serviced customers myself both on the phone and face to face, I know that providing great customer service requires energy. It's important to stay upbeat throughout the day as one's lack of energy is very noticeable to the customer (yes – a lack of energy is *very* noticeable over the phone). Notice how your prospects enter the room, how they greet you, their sitting posture during the interview and the pace of their responses to your questions. These are all tips as to the level of energy that they will bring when interacting with your customers.

4. **Hire Good Ears** – One's ability to listen well is another required trait for being successful at customer service. Good ears help one to listen for what's important to a customer. When developing a solution for a customer's need/want, good ears are critical as they allow one to ask good questions in response to the reasons the customer provides for seeking to utilize your product/services. They also assist in filtering for the real issue when the customer is upset. The need to speak should be secondary to the need to listen. Real listening requires one to focus. How well does

5. the prospect listen during the interview? When you are leading the conversation, does the prospect wait until you complete your thoughts before speaking? Does their response/questions indicate that they are actively listening when you speak? Do they maintain eye contact during the conversation? These are all indicators of one's listening ability.

6. **Hire Thinkers** – I often look back on my career in customer service and think about how often I had to be quick on my feet (and in my brain!) when working with customers. Not every situation is routine and oftentimes it's necessary to formulate resolutions quickly. The ability to determine what is required in these non-routine situations (which requires a lot of #3) and then create a plan of action is key to retaining customers Customer service personnel must be able to think their way through these situations in order to create the best solution for both the customer and the company. Give situations and scenarios to your prospects that require them to devise a plan of action.

7. **Hire Curiosity** – Asking questions is a major component of customer service as it helps one to develop the best product/service solution for the customer. Curiosity is is a good trait for customer service personnel to possess. Look for people who have questions about your company – where it's headed, what can the prospect look

forward to if chosen for the position and even questions about your history with the company.

8. **Hire Team Players** – When performing my customer service duties, I found more often than not, that my actions impacted someone else within the company. It was important to remember to not to negatively impact others when providing service to the customer. You can determine your prospect's team player level by listening for group activities when you ask about their interests. Does their work history indicate group participation? Include group scenarios in your interview sessions that get the prospect to talk about how each group member is impacted by the decisions of one person.

And Train Them Well

As a former front line customer service employee, I understand the feeling deep down inside that you may have when you're not fully prepared to properly service your customers. Training must be a top priority to insure customer satisfaction and employee confidence. I have witnessed employee training that seemed geared toward getting employees in front of (or on the phone with) the customer as quickly as possible. While this method has an apparent positive effect by providing immediate attention to the customer or meeting key performance indicator goals (calls in que or

\# of abandoned calls for example) these are what I call "false positive" metric results. If the employee in front of or on the phone with the customer does not have the proper product/service knowledge and customer service skills training, there is a three - fold effect: 1. The employee's confidence level decreases, with possibly an increase in their frustration level. 2. The customer is not provided a quality customer service experience as a result of the employee not receiving a comprehensive training experience. 3. The employee's actions may negatively impact the organization via not having a "holistic" understanding of who's/what's affected internally by their actions. While metrics may indicate all is well, trouble may be brewing both within the company and with the external customers.

To insure that your customer service personnel receive a comprehensive training experience that will allow them to provide a quality customer service experience while at the same time positively impacting the organization, here are a few suggestions:

1. Provide extensive product/service training. Allow the employee the opportunity to utilize the product/service in order to both gain self – confidence and to understand the product/service from the customer's perspective.

2. Make sure the employee gets extensive training on whatever systems are utilized when servicing the customer. Create typical scenarios that the employee will face daily to insure enough time is spent on realistic training vs. theory based training.

3. If the employee's required inputs are used by someone else within the organization, make sure the employee knows what their "finished product" (the result of their inputs) looks like and what it should contain to meet the requirements of the next person in the work process.

4. Incorporate cross-functional visits into the training program. Allow the employee to spend time with those persons impacted by the employee's daily duties and with those whose daily duties impact the employee. This promotes a "holistic" perspective throughout the organization. Where the visits are not physical possible, utilize video conferencing platforms to create a virtual visit.

5. Prepare the training attendees for the "people portion" of customer service by providing customer service skills training. This will assist in insuring that all product/service interactions are handled in a professional and customer friendly manner.

6. Survey training attendees about 30 days after their completion of the training program. Get their opinion of how effective the training proved to be after they've been in the "real world" of servicing customers. Their answers will assist in the constant evolution of the training program in its goal to provide a comprehensive training experience. As your product/service or other internal processes change, provide refresher training to maintain a high level of customer service delivery.

Customer service personnel can make or break your company. To insure that your customers receive great customer service, take the time to hire the right person to service your customers. Hire people – not just experience. Remember, the right people, delivering great service, create loyal customers, which leads to referrals, creates long term success

Exercise

1. Examine your hiring process – What attributes besides experience are you currently seeking in new hires?

2. Examine your training process. Search for areas of opportunity – Is there enough product/service knowledge training? Are cross-functional visits included? Are the trainers qualified to provide the level of training required to create "experts"? Are the trainees afforded an opportunity to give feedback on the training program?

3. Develop a hiring team. Attempt to get members with different personality strengths as this allows for the sharing of different viewpoints on prospective candidates.

Chapter 5 – Develop Fair Employee Rewards Systems

Does this sound familiar? "I can't possibly complete all of this work and meet the goals to receive a raise. It just doesn't seem fair. I don't think management understands what it takes to actually do this job". I actually heard these very words during a stint at a national corporation. The daily workload was unbearable. The performance standards were not balanced with the heavy workload. Tasks required for insuring a great customer service experience made sense, but the workload led to employees taking shortcuts in an attempt to keep from falling behind. Lunch breaks were non-existent as employees were reluctant to lose time in their attempt to keep up with the workload demands. To top it off, if someone spoke up about the working conditions, they were deemed to be a trouble maker or told "You're not a team player."

Employees today are experiencing more stress than ever in this era of economic uncertainty. It's very important to align workload and performance goals for long term positive employee morale, long term profitability and long term productivity. Your customers (both external and internal) are impacted by your performance goals. Here are a few issues to consider.

24

Performance Goals - Is That The Right Number?

When establishing performance goals, take into consideration the total process required for task completion. Base goals on outcomes over which the employee has control. Where the employee has accountability for additional tasks, factor this into goal setting for the employee's primary responsibility. This will lead to setting realistic goals. In regards to the corporation mentioned at the beginning of the chapter, there were several additional daily required tasks for employees in my position to complete. We all knew they were necessary, yet struggled to complete them as required. These tasks were not factored into the primary task performance goals. If focus was not maintained on the primary tasks, your performance results in those areas suffered. If you did maintain focus on the primary tasks, but allowed the additional daily tasks to accumulate, your performance results in these areas were impacted as well. Spend time with the employees as they actually perform their duties to get a "real world" feel for what it takes to perform the job (we'll talk about this later in more detail). Include the employees who actually perform the job in establishing goals. An environment of mutual respect will exist as the employees will feel that they were able to participate in creating their own goals. The level of service provided to the customer is higher when employees are not overly concerned and stressed out daily about meeting performance goals. Taking these steps has a three-fold effect: 1. Improvement in employee morale. 2.

You may be able to create a better process. 3. You should be able to determine if the stated goal is the right goal.

Quality Versus Quantity - Which Is Primary?

Does your reward system encourage quality work? A reward system based on unrealistic performance goals tends to promote quantity over quality. As employees struggle to meet the stated goals, quality will surely suffer as short cuts become the norm in completing tasks. This can lead to poor work audit results, rework (how much does this cost at your company?) and customer dissatisfaction. Employees are prone to display a sense of hurriedness when interacting with customers if the workload and performance goals are not balanced. Those employees choosing quality over quantity will become frustrated as their efforts to perform the job properly are rewarded with inquiries regarding their inability to reach the stated goal. In the quantity over quality environment created by unrealistic performance goals, long term productivity is sacrificed for the short term goal. Focus on systemic thinking and make this a high priority when designing reward systems. Reward actions that insure fluid cross-functional handoffs. This helps to build a culture of holistic, systemic minded employees who understand the impact of their work to the product/service system.

Work Environment - Is This A Healthy Place To Work?

It is very important to create a positive work environment as your bottom line is directly impacted by employee morale. An environment where performance goals are fair and obtainable fosters an atmosphere of teamwork as employees do not feel the need to protect their "numbers". Unrealistic goals lead to either unwillingness – for fear of not meeting their own goals or inability – due to unrealistic work load – to truly work as a team. Long term employee frustration usually results in a lower quality of work which ultimately impacts the external customer. Stress levels increase possibly leading to health issues. Employee turnover increases as well as some will seek relief from an atmosphere they deem unfair and unhealthy. This directly impacts your bottom line as the level of customer service delivered suffers via productivity lost to the need to hire and train new employees. How much does a dissatisfied customer cost your company? Promote employee quality of life versus "my work is my life" mindset. Give employees a reason to feel good about coming to work.

Performance goals and reward systems are key components of the business environment. Strive to base both on a "real world" workload. Your long term success depends on it. Your customer will feel the impact of performance goals and the workload. Balance these two in order to insure that the customer is positively impacted and gets great customer service.

Exercise

1. Examine methods utilized in creating your employee performance goals. Spend time with your employees to determine if performance goals are obtainable considering the daily workload.

2. Establish whether or not your company's performance goals foster teamwork.

3. Determine the employee turnover rate for your company. What are the top two reasons that employees leave your company?

Chapter 6 - Managing For Great Customer Service

Now that you've developed good hiring practices, trained your employees well and developed fair performance standards, it's important to develop good management practices. Customer service is impacted through methods utilized to manage employees who are servicing the customer. When employees are treated in the same manner that they are required to exhibit to the customer, the customer is the benefactor. If a gap exists between the two, the customer suffers as a higher rate of employee turnover, an attitude of indifference and other negative characteristics become apparent due to improper management techniques. As a former customer service manager, I know the position requires one to possess a balance of operational knowledge and people skills. Both are necessary in insuring the best possible experience for both team members and customers. Here are a few tips on managing this balancing act:

Remember that your employees are people. Often times as a manager, it's easy to get caught up in metrics. These are important, as they assist in advising you of the state of your operation. Your employees help drive these metrics, so your people skills are required here. Take the time to explain to your team members how they contribute to the success of the customer's experience. Always be conscious of the fact that you can't meet the metric goals without your team. Your listening skills are critical in your role as a manager. Seek out and reward ideas for improvement. Implement those that result in cost savings or have a positive impact on the metrics. Provide more positive feedback than negative feedback. If your employees receive enough positive feedback, they are better able to receive feedback that points to needed improvement. Keep team meetings based on team issues. Celebrate individual and team accomplishments. Protect the integrity of your team members by keeping individual negative performance issues in private. Find someone on the team to develop for a management position - in other words, train someone to replace you.

Develop cross functional awareness. This one is for the operational side of your skill set. As a manager, I always found it interesting and helpful to understand how other areas of the company operated. It's important to know how your operation impacts other areas within the organization and vice versa. This knowledge will help you to develop better processes within your area. Share this knowledge with your team in order to promote cross functional thinking. The goal is to get your team to say to themselves - "When I do this, who's impacted by my actions?"

Watch for patterns. - This tip has a mixture of both people and operational skills. Let's start with the operational side. As an analytical person by nature, I'm always interested in patterns which meant I spent a lot of time graphing data. What I learned by doing this is that operation metrics usually contain patterns. I found that every one of my operational metrics flowed in a pattern. Since data analysis was a fun task for me, I would graph weeks of data to identify patterns. Doing so helped me to make operational adjustments to correct a negative pattern. More importantly, it helped me not to improperly respond to "blips". "Blips" are what I considered a temporary change in the pattern that could be attributed to a one time incident - product issues, service related issues, etc. I would closely watch to make sure that the negative pattern change did not become a permanent change. Even if the pattern change is positive - it bears investigating to get the story behind the change, just to make sure that the customer still receives a great experience.

In regards to people and patterns, it has been my experience that everyone has a pattern. I found that team members usually perform their duties with their own signature - the way they converse with customers, the way they input information into systems and the way they interact with others. Just as in the example regarding operational patterns, it's important to know and monitor people patterns. A negative "blip" on the people side may be a one-time loss of call control or improper account notation. If further observations reveal no indication of repeat behavior, then consider that a "blip". Protracted negative changes in the pattern may be an indication that the team member is experiencing stress - either occupational or personal. A conversation with this team member advising them that you've noticed a change in their work pattern and give them specific examples of the change. A simple conversation like this may lead to the team member advising you of issues that are impacting their job performance. Offer the appropriate assistance within company guidelines. Your team member will feel that you care about them as a person and not just an employee. During one managerial stint, I remember listening to one of the best call center employees with the company stumble through several calls as if it was her first time on the phone. Knowing that this was not her normal pattern, I advised her that I had listened to her last several calls and that she didn't sound like herself. She advised me of some personal issues that she left home that morning without resolving. I advised her to call home and resolve the issues and come see me before resuming her duties. She took about 15 minutes to do so and appeared at my door to thank me for allowing her to take care of the unresolved issues. After resuming her duties, she was back to her normal pattern in handling her customers.

Remain objective. This tip is critical when giving feedback to your team members. Performance evaluations and coaching sessions should be based upon objective information. Provide data and examples on which the evaluation is based. Subjectivity will only lead to trouble. Team members should know that their performance rating is based upon their written performance standards which were created from the job description. Provide performance feedback on a regular basis as your team members look for consistency in this area.

Give respect to get respect. I think it's every manager's wish that they be respected as the person in charge. It's been my experience that the best way to get respect is to give respect. Respect your team members as people first. Respect what they do by spending time performing their duties. Whatever it is that they do - take calls, service customers face to face, handle customers as a field service rep - you do it with them to get a real world view of what is required to actually do the job. Ask for their opinions by using these four words - "What do you think?" Listen to their opinions regarding operational issues. Be an advocate for your team. Remove obstacles that hinder their success. Team members will respect the position when they feel that the person in that position respects them.

It takes courage to be a manager. Balance the operational side and the people side for a better long term result. I always found that it's better to manage through persuasion (here's where we're headed) vs. commandment (you're going whether you like it or not). The best compliment for me when one of my team members was asked "What do you like most about having Errol as a manager?" was their answer "He cares about us as people and he's fair." Believe or not, your customer feels the impact of your management style. Some say that employees should give the customer the best service experience no matter what the condition of the internal environment. I say that's true, but how long can you expect the employee to sustain his/her ability to do so? Manage the employee in the same manner that you expect them to service the customer.

Exercise

1. Examine your methods of developing your supervisory/managerial staff.

2. Examine your methods utilized for performance reviews. Weed out subjectivity.

3. Schedule time to spend with other functions within your organization – primarily those which impact your function and those impacted by your function.

4. Schedule time to spend with your employees individually while they perform their duties. Do so without reviewing their performance.

Chapter 7 – Leaders Spend Time on the Front Line

Before we move too far away from the last chapter, I'd like to discuss a little further why I feel it's critical that supervisors, managers and owners learn to balance their people and operational skills. One sure way to achieve this feat is to spend time on the front lines. During my career in the customer service industry, I've learned that this one adventure can act as a catalyst in the quest to provide great customer service. Okay, Okay. I hear someone asking "How is that Errol?" By choosing to visit and help out with the employees, the atmosphere starts shifting. The front line employees are amazed that you care enough about them and what they do to actually spend time doing it yourself! Employee morale is an important component in delivering great customer service and the willingness to spend time on the front line can assist in raising the employee satisfaction ratings. Your customer is on the receiving end of employee satisfaction. Often as managers and executives, the tendency to be removed from what actually happens "in the trenches" is probably more of the norm than the exception. Position requirements and expectations often monopolize much if not all of a leader's time. I suggest that leaders regularly carve out time to spend on the front lines and actually get a "hands-on" experience. Here's why:

1. Enlightenment - In today's business environment, managing by the numbers seems to be the way to go. Numbers are critical in managing a business, but one must remember there is a story and people behind the numbers. As a leader, you may be surprised to learn the "real" story. Time spent on the front line actually performing the duties connected to your numbers will assist you in determining if the numbers utilized for performance goals are in fact the correct numbers or if adjustments are required. Compare your operations numbers to your customer satisfaction levels. Is there a negative gap between the two? Your operation may appear to be successful according to the operations numbers, but if the customer satisfaction levels are not following the same pattern, it's time to get the real story. In the same manner, compare your operations numbers to your employee satisfaction levels. It's been my experience that this one can fool you. Your operations numbers and employee satisfaction levels may look good, but how's your employee turnover level? Often times employees true feelings are spoken with their feet in comparison to what they say. Regular visits to the front line will assist you in getting the real story behind the numbers.

2. Respect - The amount of respect you gain from the front line workers by spending time with them is enormous! During my last corporate stint, I challenged a vendor manager to spend time performing the work of his front line workers. I had frequent conversations with these workers and understood the imbalance of their workload and performance goals. The vendor manager responded to my challenge with a resounding "Not happening!" One day later, where was this manager? On the front, line performing the same duties as the other workers. What was their response to his being there? The word spread like wildfire! They knew that he could not perform the duties at their rate of speed, but were elated that he took the time to learn first-hand the reality of their work situation. His respect and appreciation for these workers changed after this experience. The front line workers' respect level for the manager changed as well. Hopefully, more realistic performance goals were the outcome of this scenario.

3. **Improved Morale** - Imagine the long-term effects to employee morale in the example given above regarding the vendor manager's decision to spend time working on the front lines.. When front-line workers believe that leaders care enough to "get in the trenches" to gain the front-line workers' perspective, a positive morale shift is usually close behind. A long-term positive change in morale follows if changes are instituted to assist the front-line worker in being more successful in servicing their customers (both internal and external customers). Front-line workers usually have great ideas for improvement and are just waiting for someone to ask for their opinion. Regular visits to the front-line will provide a regular flow of new ideas and suggestions.

4. Improved Customer Experience - An improved customer experience is usually the result of leaders getting hands-on experience at the front line. As leaders typically have some measure of influence within an organization, they can be the driving force behind needed changes and ideas for improvement that become evident when spending time on the front line. As these changes are implemented within the organization, a positive impact flows out to the customer through improved service and front line employee attitude and demeanor.

A front line experience is good for all leaders. It gives one a different perspective on what actually happens within an organization. I have a saying - "What you see is not always what is - ask questions - your perspective may change as a result of the answers." Don't rely solely upon numbers to run your organization. Spend some time on the front line!

Exercise

1. How often do you and or your managerial staff spend time on the front line.?

2. How well does your managerial staff understand the day to day operations?

3. If you asked both a front line employee and someone from the managerial staff the same operational question are you confident that you would get the same response?

Chapter 8 - Create Customer/Employee Friendly Processes

In the last two chapters we discussed the importance of exercising good management skills – from both the people and operational perspectives. Now let's give these people a reason to stay and feel good about servicing the customer. Always remember that customer service is a people oriented business. Don't forget that your employees are people first. You can have the most modern facilities, with all of the bells and whistles and it won't mean anything if your employees are unhappy. All of the modern tools to monitor and evaluate employee performance will be regarded as weapons by employees if they feel that the work environment is unhealthy.

During my customer service career, one of the most frustrating experiences was attempting to service the customer while working within a system that was neither customer nor employee friendly. Doing so makes for a long day, which when repeated over a long period of time, can drain the life from even the best customer service personnel. Inefficient processes create a double-edged sword: frustrated customers and frustrated employees. Here's a process related story for you. While employed as an operations analyst for a major telecommunications company, my normal path through the building often took me directly past the area where walk-in customers visited to make bill payments. It seemed that the line was more often long than short. Now most people who know me know that long lines set off an alarm in my head. After making the decision to spend an entire day with the employees in this area, the reason for the long lines became evident real fast. The employees were writing receipts for customers – even though printers were installed at each work station.

The workers advised me that they were only allowed to utilize the printers for the high volume of walk-in traffic before a pay-per-view event. So does that mean that the regular walk-in customer is not important? I inquired at the next managers meeting, as to when was the last time a manager spent any time in this particular work area. The question was met with silence. To make a long story short, the printers were turned on for everyday usage resulting in happier employees and no more long lines for the customer. This one simple change in the walk-in payment process changed the experience for both the employee and the customer. It's important to develop work processes that serve both the internal customer (employees) and the external customer (those who purchase your product/service) well. Here are a few tips on developing efficient processes.

1. **Identify all participants and stakeholders in your processes.** – The creation of great processes requires the participation of all parties involved in the process. Process participants are those who actually touch and or are impacted by the process. Stakeholders on the other hand may be entities that hold your business to a certain standard. City ordinances, licensing agencies and legal entities are just a few

41

examples of external stakeholders that may require you to do things in a certain manner. Auditors are one example of an internal stakeholder that impacts your processes.

When facilitating process improvement projects, it's always fun to witness the change in group dynamics. Where there may have been a level of apprehension amongst the group members at the beginning of the project, more than likely, the apprehension is replaced with understanding and agreement. Employees become more team-oriented when they understand how they impact one another when performing day to day duties and when working together to improve the work environment.

2. **Identify the steps in the process.** - Begin by mapping the process as it currently exists – step by step – with the participants providing input on their particular contribution to the process. At this stage, you're not looking to identify issues and solutions; you just want to get the process out in the open for all to see. Once this is done and all participants agree "yes this is what happens during this particular process", you're ready to begin creating a more efficient process.

3. **Identify opportunities for improvement.** Now it's time to identify unnecessary steps (waste), determine if current technology can assist in improving the process, or verify if parts of the process can be done in parallel (at the same time). This will assist in developing an employee and customer friendly process.

4. Identify the financial impact of inefficient processes. – How much does rework cost in your business? Rework is required when errors are made in servicing your customer. The order does not contain the correct number of items. Your customer received the item in the wrong size and color! The finished product does not meet the specifications given by the customer. These are all examples of moments when you will be in a situation where rework is required. Get the calculator out and determine what rework costs in real dollars. How much is yours and your employees' time worth? If your time is worth $75.00 per hour and it takes you two hours to correct an issue that totals $150.00.

Don't forget that you could have utilized those two hours on a revenue generating activity. So that's an additional $150.00 that's been lost to rework. If materials costs are involved in correcting the issue, the total cost of rework can quickly escalate. Take the time to determine the financial impact of rework on your business. Now don't forget how much your customers are worth. If non-customer friendly processes cause you to lose customers, add this to the financial impact. Inefficient processes may result in the loss of employees as well. Remember how much you spend on hiring properly, training properly and benefits such as health insurance.

5. Develop a new efficient process. – With all of the information gained during this exercise, this next step should be fun! You've identified what the existing process looks like, opportunities for improvement have been uncovered and you understand the financial impact of rework. So now all of the process participants can build a more efficient process that meets the requirements of all stakeholders and is both customer and employee friendly.

6. **Develop the process from your customer's perspective.** – Become the customer to get an understanding of what the customer experiences when participating in the process. Where does the process begin for the customer? For example, when you go to the grocery store, where does your experience begin? Some may say it begins when you enter the store. In my opinion your experience begins when you enter the parking lot. Is the lot clean, are the parking spots free of empty shopping carts. I like to get a basket before I enter the store. Are there baskets available at the entrance to the store? Where does the process begin for your customer? Spend time in your customer's shoes to identify where the experience begins.

7. **Measure the effectiveness of the process.** – Now that you've taken the time to develop an efficient process, make sure to measure its effectiveness. Choose important points to track – Is the process completed in a more timely fashion than the original process? Are inputs into the process meeting the requirements of those persons utilizing the inputs? Is rework an issue? If so, how often and at what cost? Establish how often to review the process to insure that it maintains a positive pattern of operation.

Hopefully, you can see why it's necessary to examine your processes. The impact of efficient processes to the success of your business creates the need to always be in the mindset of "how can you improve this process?" and "are our processes both customer and employee friendly?" The time taken to examine your processes will pale in comparison to the positive impact to your business through customer and employee retention.

Exercise

1. Identify a process within your organization that impacts your external customer.

2. Map out each step of the process step by step.

3. Examine your process for opportunities for improvement.

4. Make the necessary changes.

5. Measure the process in order to be able to calculate the post change results.

6. Determine the financial impact of the changes.

Chapter 9 - Be Accessible & Responsive

Now that we've spent time in the previous chapters discussing internal requirements for for delivering great customer service, let's turn the focus to customer interactions. During the early years of my customer service career, there were only three contact methods (channels) utilized by the customer when attempting to reach a business: telephone, snail mail or a physical visit to your location. That's certainly changed! In addition to these channels, we now have email, online chat, website, and the various social media channels – **Facebook, Twitter**, and **LinkedIn**. Oh yeah – don't forget that your customer can use all of these channels (and others) to spread either good or bad news about your business. Let's talk about your customer's first impression when visiting your business and then we'll go on to discuss how important it is to be accessible and responsive when your customer attempts to reach you.

When Your Customer Visits Your Business

What does your customer see when they visit your business? Perception is everything! Remember, your customer's experience with your business begins when they arrive at your location. How's the exterior look? What's the condition of your signage? Don't forget the parking lot. Is it clean? All of these are key factors in your customer's first impression of your business.

Imagine yourself as a customer and your efforts to do business with a company go unnoticed or unacknowledged. How do you feel when you enter an establishment and it seems that no one cares. Here's a quick story. When I decided to take up photography as a hobby several years ago, I visited a local camera store with the hope of purchasing a camera. Well, I was in the store for 10 minutes without being acknowledged or asked if I needed any assistance. There weren't very many customers in the store, just a few people milling around like me. I thought to myself "It appears they don't need my money so I'll get out of their way." A few miles away is another camera store where my presence was acknowledged as soon as I opened the door. This is now the only camera store that I use for my photography needs!

When your customer enters your business, you have about five seconds to acknowledge their presence. You may find yourself engaged with another customer, which is understandable, but acknowledge the entering customer as well. Most people are reasonable and will understand that you're already engaged with someone, but an acknowledgement is still in order. Make eye contact when acknowledging your customer's presence. Ever walk into an establishment where it seems all of the employees yell out "Welcome to......!!" yet none make eye contact? This is what I refer to as a scripted acknowledgement. Heard but not felt. I hear your acknowledgement, but you're not making me feel appreciated because you won't even look at me.

After acknowledging their presence, be available for assistance. All customers don't always need assistance, but for those that do, it's imperative that help is not very far away. Bring you expert knowledge with you as your customer deserves your best efforts. Ask questions in order to create the proper solution for your customer. When interacting with your customer, be aware of your body language. Don't send the wrong signals with your facial expressions. Beware of giving the impression that the customer is interrupting you. Serve sincerely. Stay away from the "point and tell" method of guiding your customer to a specific item. Choose the "take and assist" method instead which requires one to take the customer to the item and when appropriate, assist them in choosing the items that fits their need. Your customer can see and feel if you really care about them. Let's talk about what to do when your customer calls your business.

When Your Customer Calls Your Business

I thought about approaching several business related magazines in regards to submitting articles for consideration. After an unsuccessful search of the website of a well-known national magazine for their article submission criteria, I decided to just call the magazine's publishing company. The person answering the phone was pleasant, listened to my reason for calling and advised me that it would be necessary to transfer my call to the appropriate person. The next person answered right away, listened to my request, then stated that the article submission criteria could be found on their website by entering Pitch To Us in the search area. I was in the middle of asking her if she could hang on with me while I followed her instructions on the website, but didn't get the chance to finish my request because she stated "Uh no. I have to go! and disconnected the call. I sat in stunned silence for about a minute before sharing the ordeal with my wife who burst into laughter!

Have you ever called a business and at the end of the call, you were not happy with the experience? Take a moment and write down the reasons why you felt unhappy. Examine your own inbound call process to insure that they don't contain the same negative elements. Here's what I suggest to you regarding providing customer service when your customer calls your business.

Answer the phone in a timely manner – this means within one to three rings. This applies to all size businesses – from the one person operation to the large corporations. Your customer expects you to be available when they need you. There are times when you are unable to answer the phone as you may find yourself in a meeting or on the phone with a customer. If you're a one person operation, utilize a good voice mail message to advise the customer when they can expect a return call, along with other contact options. Return your customer's call within your specified time frame (I suggest same business day). You might say, "Errol, I'm just a small company. Do I really need to go to that extent?" I would suggest that you go ahead and act like the big company that you hope to become.

What does your customer expect if you're a larger company? Have you ever heard someone say "You'd think that as big as they are, their service would be much better than it is!" The larger your company, the greater your customer's expectations regarding your availability by phone. Having spent many years in the call center environment, I know firsthand how customers react to typical call center scenarios. Customers don't particularly like to be placed on hold without their permission ("Thank you for calling...Hold please!"), are not happy with being placed on hold for extended periods, don't want to hear your on-hold music; aren't particularly happy with the Interactive

Voice Response (IVR) process (that's the voice that says "For English press one") and absolutely hate the blind transfer as it makes them start over again as to why they called in the first place. Okay, let's tackle each scenario.

Always get the customer's permission before placing them on hold. When it is necessary to place a customer on hold, advise them of the anticipated time that they will be on hold and come back to refresh the call within that time frame.

There are situations where a call transfer is necessary. If there is a specific person to whom you will be transferring the call, attempt to reach the person to advise them of the reason for the customers' call to allow them to mentally prepare for the call. If the person is unavailable, advise the customer and ask if they would like to be transferred to leave a voice mail message. If you're transferring to a department where multiple persons can provide assistance, attempt to reach someone before transferring the call. Before transferring, advise the customer as to who will be providing assistance. Always provide your direct phone information just in case you're accidentally disconnected from the customer (This does happen sometimes!) Always thank the customer for calling and for being a customer.

Make sure that your IVR is customer friendly. How can I do this Errol? Simple, you become the customer. Call your own company and utilize the IVR. Are the options customer friendly? Are the instructions easy to follow? Call companies where you have accounts and follow the IVR instructions. How does their system compare to yours? What do you like? What don't you like? What about theirs can be incorporated into yours to create a better customer experience? Utilize IVR data to identify why customers are opting out to a live person. The goal is for customers choosing to utilize the IVR to be able to complete their visit within the IVR. These points should help you be ready when your customer calls. We have another channel to check – your website.

When Your Customer Visits Your Website

I received this customer service story from a member of a local organization here in Houston, Texas. This member volunteers as a liaison between new members and the organization. She received a phone call from a new member regarding the location for an organizational committee meeting. It appears that the new member was at the wrong location. The liaison member conferenced the new member to the organization's phone number in an attempt to get the correct meeting location. When the new member advised the organization's receptionist of her dilemma, the receptionist asked "Where did you get that information?". The new member advised the receptionist that the information was retrieved from the organization's website. The receptionist then asked "When did you get the information?" to which the new member responded "A few days ago." The receptionist responded "Well that's the wrong information." The new member already knew this! The receptionist then stated "We only update the information on the website once a month!" The liaison member was still on the line and interjected at this point with the question "Wait a minute. Are you saying you knew the information was wrong on the website, but you didn't update it?" The receptionist again stated "We only update the website once a month." She then proceeded to provide the correct meeting address in such a rapid manner that the new member had to ask for the address to be repeated. The call ended without an apology to the new member for the error and the inconvenience.

When your customer visits your business through your website, what should they expect? In regards to the story at the beginning of this chapter, customers expect your information to be current. If the organization's website was updated in a timely manner with the correct event location, there would not have been a need for the phone call. Additionally customers look for ease of use. It's similar to a visit to your physical location. Can they find what they're looking for? How many pages does your customer have to negotiate before finding the needed information? Can they search within your website for products/services? Make sure all of your links work properly. Your customer should be able to contact you from your website either via email of web chat. In regards to your email, utilize an auto-responder to insure the customer that you know that they are attempting to reach you. Include information on when they can expect to hear from you. When your customer orders services or products via your website, make sure your auto-responder provides a delivery date, shipment tracking information, a phone number on how to reach your company to check the status of the delivery and a product/service guarantee.

If your company is large enough to warrant giving your customer the option of web chat, provide this feature as it gives your customer another avenue for "live" contact with your business. During interaction with the customer via this channel, act as though you were actually on the phone with the customer. Ask for permission to pause when the need arises. Refresh your pauses so as not to give the impression that you are no longer chatting. Insure that the customer's question has been answered or their issue is resolved before ending the chat. Thank the customer for chatting. Take a look at your competitors' website. Find features that you like and would make sense for your customers.

When Your Customer Emails You

While conducting a customer service workshop, I raised a question regarding responding to customer emails. "How many of you have an email response strategy for your business?" Silence – no hands raised was the response to the question. I posed another question – "How long does it take you to respond to customer (existing or prospective) emails?" "Forty – eight hours!" was one reply. I asked one final question "How long can it take your customer to locate someone else to provide the same service/product that you offer?"

Email is another contact channel that's available to your customer. Develop a response strategy for this channel. What's your response time? 1 hour, same business day? I would suggest no later than the same business day. An email that goes without a response is like an unreturned phone call. When you are unavailable to respond to emails, utilize your auto-responder to advise your customer and provide information as to when you will respond to emails. Where your company is a large company and you are unable to handle the tasks requested in your customer's email, utilize the transfer techniques discussed earlier regarding transferring phone calls: 1. Advise the appropriate party of the need to refer the request/issue to them. Give a brief description of the

57

request/issue and steps that have already been taken regarding the matter. 2. Advise the customer of the need to refer them to the appropriate party, giving the person's name and contact information.

Treat emails just as you would a phone call. Answer promptly. Address your customer's concerns. When it's necessary to gather information before responding, act as though you are placing the customer on hold during a phone call. Advise them of your need to gather more information and set an expectation as to when you will follow up. Ask the customer if they are in agreement with your plan. Remember, email is just another form of conversation. When utilizing email, act as though the customer is standing right in front of you. Just as you would promptly acknowledge a customer's presence, do the same when you receive an email. Your customer's perception is "I sent you an email so I know you will see it shortly." Develop an email response strategy to insure your customer feels great about your ability to communicate .

Three Ways To Get Your Customer To Help You Provide Great Customer Service

In addition to being available and responsive, it's important to get your customer to assist you in providing great customer service. Yes I hear you asking "How am I supposed to do that Errol?" Glad you asked! Here's three ways to get this done.

Tell your customers what you need them to provide: It has often been my experience that if I had been advised of what was needed when calling or visiting certain business, the interaction may have been more efficient for both me and the customer service employee. Post contact requirements on your website's contact us page, on your snail mail information, in your emails when appropriate, in your IVR, at customer service counters, and other contact points. If your customer has an appointment to visit your business, advise them of what they should bring in order to make the experience a positive one. Doing so prompts your customer to have all of the necessary information readily available, which in turn assists the customer contact personnel in promptly and efficiently servicing the customer. Before having minor knee surgery a couple of years ago, I was advised by a representative from the surgical facility what information and documents to bring when arriving the morning of the surgery. The interaction was very smooth and efficient upon my arrival for surgery.

59

Tell your customers what you need them to do: Recently I visited the post office to retrieve a certified document. I stood in the line for 10 minutes before catching a glimpse of a sign stating - "Customers picking up certified mail form a line here." The sign was located behind, to the left and above the front counter, in a recessed storage area, thereby increasing the possibility of one not seeing it when entering the post office. I would recommend placing the sign near the post office entrance and once again at the entrance to the main area where most transactions take place. This would aid the customer in going to the proper counter, thereby eliminating unnecessary time spent in the wrong line. Strategically placed signage assists your customer in going to proper locations for service. Anxiety and frustration levels tend to rise when the customer is not sure where they need to be when entering your facility.

Make sure the signage is clear and understandable. During a visit a few months ago to a local car wash, I noticed the signage had changed, but the new signage was a little confusing. As I pulled forward and asked the attendant which line was the correct line for someone on my specific wash program, he bluntly stated that the information was on the sign. After reminding him that I can read, but the signage was a little confusing, he gruffly advised me that I was in fact in the correct line. In both situations, a little time taken to become the customer in regards to the sign location and language may have prevented the negative interactions. By the way, the car wash employee was the recipient of my "Secret Service Agent" stare after his remarks.

Tell your customers how to help themselves - Not all customers require the personal touch. Some prefer to do things themselves - not necessarily because they fear the level of service they may receive when interacting with customer service personnel - it's just their preference. When a customer chooses to utilize your "self-service" channels, make sure that instructions are readily available. Place clear instructions on your website, in your IVR and at your self-service counters. Make it a point to regularly check your self-service systems to insure smooth functionality for your customer. Once again, become the customer to make sure your instructions are clear and to insure your systems are customer friendly.

Your customer depends upon you for a great customer experience. Get them to assist you in doing so by proactively: 1. **Telling them what they need to provide. 2. Telling them what they need to do. 3. Telling them how to help themselves.** They will appreciate your attention to detail and your front line employees will benefit as well via increased interaction efficiency.

Exercise

Become the customer and do the following (where it's applicable):

1. Drive up to your business as if you are a customer.

2. Call your business regularly to see how long before the phone is answered.

3. Visit your website as if you are a customer. Order something (if applicable).

4. Visit your business as if you are a customer. Examine your customer touch points.

5. Are there any apparent opportunities for improvement?

Chapter 10 - Properly Assess Your Customer's Needs

The method that I've found helpful in assessing a customer's need is one that I'll call the "Who, What, When, Where, How and Why method. This format requires one to ask questions to gain understanding. Understanding leads to providing the best solution for your customer. It may not be necessary to utilize all of the questions in every situation, but I've found that this method encourages your customer to elaborate about their need. A customer visiting a garden center to purchase flowers and gardening equipment may require the garden center employee to utilize the following components:

Where are you building the flower bed? **How** is that location impacted by sunlight? **What** type of flowers are you interested in purchasing? The customer's response to these questions helps the employee to utilize his/her expertise in making recommendations that will insure a good outcome (a healthy, flourishing flower bed) for the customer. Should the customer in fact have a good outcome, trust enters the picture. The employee's recommendations led to the creation of numerous daily pleasant experiences for the customer via the flourishing flower bed. The customer more than likely will lean toward consulting with this employee for future gardening needs.

Here's a story of the Who, What, When, Where, How and Why method in action. Just as in the example given regarding the garden center interaction, most of us have experienced working on a project or hobby and having the need for an item, but not quite knowing exactly what the right item might be to accomplish the end result. I myself was in this situation while preparing for a photo project. I could see in my mind what I wanted to accomplish, but didn't know which lens would give me the best result. Well, off I went to my favorite camera store (remember them?) for some help. Upon arriving and explaining my dilemma, I was asked several questions: What is the lighting like at the site of the project? How many people are involved? What time of day will the photo shoot take place? What type of photos will you take – action, portraits? What the camera store employee was doing is what I call assessing my needs. He was asking questions to gather information in order to properly fulfill my need. He then offered lens options along with typical camera settings for my photo project. That's why this is the only camera store that I do business with – they're concerned that I purchase the items to fit my need versus just trying to make a sale.

This is a simple but effective method to properly assess the needs of your customers. Ask open-end questions that allow your customer to elaborate. You have a better chance of being successful in meeting the needs of your customers.

Exercise

1. What methods are you and your employees utilizing to assess what your customer wants and needs?

2. How well do you and your employees know your products or services?

3. Is customer needs assessment included in your training program?

Chapter 11 - Clarify and Meet Your Customer's Expectations

I believe most if not all of us have participated in the drive-thru experience at our favorite fast food restaurant. You pull up to the ordering station and someone asks (hopefully quickly) if they can take your order. As you place your order, it appears on the screen, which gives you an opportunity to make sure that your order is placed properly. Most often, the restaurant employee will repeat your order to make sure they heard you correctly. Once the okay is given that yes, your order has been taken properly, you proceed to the window to make payment and retrieve your order. This is where the rubber meets the road. If you're like me, you check your order to verify that it's correct. If it is, you go on your way. If not, then here comes the rework! This is a simple example of clarifying what the customer expects to receive and then making sure to follow through.

After spending time to assess your customer's needs as we discussed in the previous chapter, it is most important to clarify the expectation. This gives both you and your customer the opportunity to discuss what the customer expects to receive. This conversation should include the details – what is expected, when can the customer expect to receive it, how will you deliver it to the customer and what should the customer expect to pay, what payment methods are available and so on. You must get this one right, as your reputation depends upon your ability to consistently do so. If your customer can order from your website, give them the opportunity to verify that their selections are indeed what they intend to purchase. Most product oriented websites such as Amazon allow customers to review their selections to insure the items in the cart are in actuality what the customer wants and are in the correct quantity. Can your customer do the same on your website? Your attention to clarifying expectations is both proactive and preventive.

Proactive in the sense that your customer can see your attention to detail in regards to making sure that you properly fulfill their need/want. Preventive as it lessens the chance that you will not meet your customer's expectations. Should this happen, you will find yourself in the customer recovery mode. Your being is the mode will surely cost money, as the need to correct an issue – also known as rework – arises in order to satisfy your customer. How much does rework cost you? If your time is worth $125.00 an hour and it takes two hours to correct the issue. Well that equals $250.00. Hold on. The time spent correcting that issue could have been utilized to service another customer. So that's an additional $250.00 lost to rework. Now let's add any material costs to this equation, for simplicity sake $100.00. You spent an initial $100.00 to provide your product/service to the customer and because of rework; you may have to tack on an additional $100.00 of material during the rework process. If that's the case, you're out $200.00 in material costs. Rather quickly you've incurred $700.00 in rework costs and possibly a blow to your business reputation. Your business success depends upon your ability to consistently clarify your customer's expectations and then meet them. Let's talk about why consistency is important.

One of the primary reasons that I continue to do business with certain establishments is that they execute in a consistent manner. It doesn't matter if I have visited the establishment 4 or 40 times, the level of service remains the same. I can depend on receiving A++ customer service. Customers want the comfort of knowing that when they visit (in person or online) or call your business, their experience will be positive every time. The ability to consistently provide great customer service has a major impact on customer retention and customer loyalty. How is consistency created? Here are a few key ingredients:

1. **Business culture** – We talked about this one in Chapter 1. Leadership must make the decision to establish a culture that focuses on consistently delivering a quality product/service and visibly "walk the talk".

2. **A good comprehensive employee training program**. - One particular establishment that I frequent appears to be good at effectively training its employees. This particular business utilizes college students as employees resulting in faces changing from time to time. The service does not suffer from this turnover as I have never experienced poor customer service in the four + years that I've been a customer. Make sure the

employee understands the overall goal (great customer service), has the product/service knowledge along with a thorough understanding of the tools (systems) required to consistently deliver a great customer service experience.

3. **Feedback** - Solicit feedback from both employees and the customers. It has been my experience that the employees have ideas on how to improve the customer service experience, they're just waiting for someone to ask for ideas. Create an environment where the employees feel safe in offering ideas for improvement. Always take time to get your customers' opinion of your service. There may be blind spots that you're not yet aware of and your customers' feedback can assist in closing that gap. We'll talk about getting customer feedback later in Chapter 18.

Consistency in service delivery is a sure way to create loyal customers who become your external marketing department - they'll advertise your product/service for you - creating additional revenue for your organization.

Exercise

1. Determine how much rework costs in your organization. Remember to consider both labor and material costs.

2. Determine the rework rate within your organization. How often are you doing things over in order to please your customer?

3. Determine if there is a pattern to your rework requests. What is the largest contributor to rework requests?

Chapter 12 – Customize When Necessary

Because customer service is a people oriented industry, you will get special requests from your customers. These special requests require some form of customization. Customization can be defined as the provision of an item or service not offered via the standard product or service listings. In some of the simplest forms this could mean substituting items in a meal, mixing products – six yellow/six orange where the norm is to ship one color per container or shipping an item to arrive on a specific date. After moving into my present home, I wanted to have an alarm system installed. As the neighborhood was new at the time, an alarm system salesman was often nearby signing up new homeowners. I quickly signed up and was given an installation date. The installer arrived, surveyed my home and was ready to begin the process. He advised me that the downstairs keypad would be located on the living room wall near the front door. As I was not fond of the idea of seeing the keypad on the wall, I made a customization request – "Can you install the keypad in the garage please?" The installer paused for a moment before saying "Let me check Mr. Allen." Within a short time he advised me that yes he could oblige my request. You see my home was prewired for the alarm system. He could pull the keypad wiring out through the wall in the garage instead of pulling the wiring the opposite direction into the living room. Your willingness to customize has its benefits. Here are several:

1. **Your customer can see that you're really interested in meeting their needs.** When you customize for your customer, you are showing your willingness to meet their special needs. Customers tend to be more loyal, when their special requests are met with a can do attitude.

2. **Your confidence level increases as you become adept at handling customization requests.** Customization creates a sense of "Yes, we can handle that!" within your organization. You may be the only one in your industry that exhibits a willingness to customize for your customer. The confidence level rises as you are able to meet your customer's customization requests.

3. **It has a positive impact on your customer retention rate.** I don't know about you, but I usually return to businesses which are willing to fulfill my special requests. Your willingness to customize virtually eliminates the competition. As long as you can consistently meet your customer's customization needs, the thought of utilizing

your competitor is non-existent. Your customer may even be willing to pay a premium for customization.

4. It prevents the chances of conflict becoming a factor. Consider a time when you requested a product be customized to fit your need. Let's keep it simple. If your request that an entrée be substituted for another at your favorite restaurant was met with "We can't do that." or "Sorry, that's not on the menu." how would you respond to that? Some people would ask "Why not?" which potentially puts the employee on the defensive which can lead to conflict. This seems like a simple request so why not just honor it. Doing so creates a loyal customer who's sure to tell others about your willingness to honor special requests.

You may need to determine the cost effectiveness of customizing to meet your customer's needs. Where it's determined that you can do so without creating a negative financial impact, consider customization. It's a great way to build brand loyalty.

Exercise

1. Establish with everyone within your organization when it's okay to customize for a customer.

2. Determine what your customization rate is.

3. On which of your products or services do you receive the majority of your customization requests.

4. Call or visit your competitor and make a customization request. What was their response?

Chapter 13 - Communicate! Keep Your Customer Informed

I remember once having to take my car in for repairs. The automotive repair facility is near my home and the owner is a personal friend. The vehicle's issue was diagnosed and I was told it would be ready in two to three hours. No problem. I called my wife to pick me up for the return trip home. When the allotted time passed without a phone call from the repair shop, I called to check on the status of my vehicle. The mechanic said in a nonchalant manner, "Your car won't be ready until tomorrow. The parts won't arrive until then." Now I can understand how repair time can be impacted by parts availability. What did not sit well with me was that I had to call to find out that my vehicle was not going to be ready as promised. When asked why I wasn't called with this information, the mechanic responded with "Someone would have called you eventually." Now that's the wrong thing to say to a customer service consultant!

Remember to keep your customers advised of task progress. Whether it's preparing your customer's meal, completing a week long task or provide shipment updates, regularly update your customer with a progress report. Establish a timeframe for updates and make sure you're proactively providing information to your customer. Ask your customer which method of notification do they prefer – phone call, email or text message. The moment that your customer has to ask for an update, you are prime for the question "Why didn't you advise me of the situation?" Your customer wants you to be proactive in informing them of delays, missed deadlines and other issues which may prevent your keeping the agreed upon commitment. Most customers are reasonable and will understand that issues do arise which are beyond your control.

The notification method may vary for problem situations. When an issue arises and your customer is on location, it's pretty easy – just provide a face to face update. In those situations where your customer is not available for face to face notification, I suggest you contact them by phone. Text messaging is another communication option. Utilize email as a backup, not primary method of notification. Your customer will feel better about a "live voice" notification versus an email which may appear cold and uncaring. Whenever there's a need to communicate bad news, it's always better for the customer to at least hear a voice. It just feels more personal when handled in this manner.

I remember watching a boxing match between a pure boxer and a brawler. As the fight began, the pure boxer kept his jab pumping to protect himself from the brawler. At the end of the round, his trainer calmly repeated "You be first. If you allow him to be first, you'll lose points. You be first." The trainer knew that it was important that his boxer be proactive during the match in order to be declared the winner. Round after round – "You be first." The same strategy applies with your customer. Proactively communicate with your customers to make them feel good about doing business with your company. Make sure they see how you feel about their choice to utilize your products/service. Establish communication strategies within your company so that your customer won't hear from you what I was told by the mechanic: 'Someone would have called you eventually." Don't lose points with your customer. **You be first**!

Exercise

1. Review your operation to insure that notification procedures are in place.'

2. What notification method do the majority of your customers choose?

3. Are you able to determine how many of your customer complaints are the result of not being advised of progress?

4. What's your response when you feel that a service provider is not providing updates in a timely fashion?

Chapter 14 – Establish Relationships With Your Customers

Do you remember meeting someone that you really liked? The more you thought about that person, the more you wanted to spend time with them. You couldn't wait to see that person! Your anticipation level was high! You wanted to make sure you looked good, smelled good and your breath was fresh. All of this because you wanted to hopefully establish a relationship with this person. You were on your best behavior, wanting to make a good impression every time the two of you met. You called this person (sometimes two or three times a day) to let them know that you were just thinking about them. Extra effort was given just for the sake of the relationship. You asked questions and listened well to learn more about the other person. Issues that are important to this person become important to you – birthdays, anniversary dates and other

How many of you realize that this describes your relationship with your customers? The relationship begins either the moment your customer contacts you or the moment you solicit your customer regarding your product or service. It's important to gather as much information as you can about your customer. Doing so assists you in starting effective and relevant conversations with your customer. Develop a customer database to assist you in developing a relationship with your customer. Purchase patterns, product or service choices, birthdays, anniversaries are some of the items that should be gathered and tracked. What's important to your customer should be a priority for you. Use your database to establish which customers' experience might be enhanced by your new product or service offerings. When repeat customers break their normal purchase pattern, contact them to determine the reason for the shift in buying habits. An opportunity to improve your business may lurk beneath the change in your customer's purchasing behavior.

When the opportunity presents itself, spend time just talking with your customers about their interests, hobbies and other topics. This is really helpful when your customers are walk-in or call-in repeat customers. What you learn during these conversations is priceless. Your customers will be amazed when you initiate conversations regarding their interests. During my last corporate stint, I met with customers face to face on a daily basis. When a customer would arrive with their vehicle bearing the state of Michigan license plates, my conversation usually started with "Spartan or Wolverine?" You see my all-time favorite college football team is the Michigan Wolverines. Their in state rivals are the Michigan State Spartans. It really didn't matter which of the two colleges they attended or maybe a fan of, it was a way for me to start a conversation. After beginning the relationship in this way, it was more often than not, a happy one throughout the life of the relationship.

You might say, "I don't see my customers Errol. They buy from me online or my business utilizes customer service reps to speak to the customer over the phone. There're still opportunities to establish a relationship. Gather as much information as possible when your customer signs up for your service or decides to purchase your product. Consider purchasing a customer relationship management product that allows this information to populate for your customer service reps to see when interacting with your customer. This allows them to ask questions such as "I see you purchased (whatever that product/service might be). How did that work for you? Did it meet your expectations?" That allows your customer to give their opinion which is important in any relationship. "I see you've been a customer with us since 2008. Thank you for your loyalty!" Now your customer feels appreciated, which may lead to more purchases in the future. Just as you would do what is necessary to establish a relationship with that person who caught your eye, do the same with your customers. Your long term success depends on it!

Exercise

1. How does your company capture information about your customer?

2. How do you utilize the information?

3. Is your customer information available to your customer contact personnel?

4. Are your customer contact personnel trained to utilize this information during customer interactions?

Chapter 15 - Create A Thank You System

The software that I utilize for creating my newsletter is a very simple program. It was easy, even for me, to choose the layout, colors and add content. While having lunch with friends about a week after signing up for the software, my phones rings and guess who's on the line? To my surprise, it was the software company calling to thank me for my purchase and to ask if everything was working out with my usage of the software. "Mr. Allen, we just wanted to thank you for choosing us to create your newsletter. Were you able to create your newsletter? Do you have any questions at this time? Well if you ever need us, call us at 1-800...... or utilize the chat feature while you're online. Thanks again for choosing us!"

Now I don't know about you, but I'm more prone to utilize products/services where the owner, managers or employees express their appreciation for my being a customer. Here's what I like to hear: 'Thanks Mr. Allen for visiting us today!" or "As a valued loyal customer, here's 20% off of your next purchase!" Does your company make it priority to be consistent about showing appreciation to your customers? How many ways can you say "Thank You"?

One that every business should employ is thanking the customer at the point of purchase. Whether the customer purchases face-to-face or online an immediate "Thank You" is appropriate and necessary. Your customers have choices! Make sure they know you are grateful that they chose to allow your business to meet their needs.

Another way to say "Thank You!" is by creating a loyalty program. Loyalty programs offer discounts to your customers in an attempt to incent them to remain loyal to your company. Make it a priority to regularly remind your loyal customers that you appreciate their business. Utilize email, text messaging, snail mail and other methods to communicate your appreciation. This is where your database is crucial. You should be able to easily identify your loyal customers from sales data.

For regular communication with your customers, develop a Thank You schedule to insure that your customer receives reminders of how much you appreciate their business. I would suggest quarterly communication just to say Thank You! Call them! Email Them! Visit Them! Send birthday greetings. Send wedding anniversary greetings! Say "Thank You!" when your customer reaches a year of doing business with you. Remember your database you created? It should contain enough information in order for you to create an effective Thank You system.

Customers want to know that their choice to do business with you is appreciated. Incorporate saying "Thank You" throughout your company. Make sure that everyone within your company understands the importance of establishing methods to say these two simple, but important words – "Thank You!"

Exercise

1. How many ways does your company say "Thank You!"?

2. How often does your company say "Thank You!"?

3. Is "Thank You" indoctrinated into your corporate culture?

4. Are leaders seen thanking the customer?

Chapter 16 – The Disgruntled Customer

There is a person that many businesses fear like the plague - the disgruntled customer. The disgruntled customer is that person who is not happy with your product/service and doesn't mind letting you know how he/she feels either via phone call, face to face or social media. Did you know that this customer is your best friend? I can hear you saying "Come on now Errol, my best friend? How can that be when they're not happy with my product/service?" Just like your best friend should be honest enough to tell you about your blind spots, the disgruntled customer - by way of their discontentment - brings your "business blind spots" to your attention. Remember, only 4% of customers that decide to stop doing business with you bother to tell you why they're no longer your customer. The other 96% just silently go away.

How do you deal with your disgruntled customer? Here are a few tips that you can use. They apply to both small and large businesses.

Listen to the issue - Allow your customer to fully vent, all the while filtering the conversation for bits of information that point to the customer's reason for disgruntlement. Let the customer know that you're listening by periodically offering a verbal confirmation such as -" I understand your frustration" or "I can understand why this is an issue for you." If your customer says "Are you still there?" (if you're on the phone with the customer) then you know that your customer feels you aren't listening. When face to face with your customer, this should never be in question!

Apologize - Offer a sincere apology for the issue. "First of all, let me apologize for any discomfort, inconvenience (whatever is appropriate) that this has caused.

Restate the issue - Repeat back to the customer what he/she stated is the cause of his/her unhappiness. This step reinforces in the customer's mind that you're really listening.

Focus on the resolution - Stay focused on the resolution. Advise your customer of what you will do to correct the situation. Ask if the resolution is acceptable. Your customer will appreciate this as you are getting their buy-in to your efforts to resolve the issue. If the customer insists on continuing to be focused on the issue, advise them again that you understand, restate your resolution and ask " May I get started on correcting this for you?" or state "Let's get started on taking care of this for you."

When you need more info - If you don't have a resolution readily available (this does happen sometimes), advise the customer that you will get the information required to develop the best resolution. Give the customer a timeframe (5 minutes, one day, etc.) in which you will provide the resolution, get their agreement and follow-up within the agreed upon timeframe. Your credibility is at stake as well as your ability to retain this customer.

Follow-up - Don't forget to follow-up with your disgruntled customer. Thank them for bringing the issue to your attention. Let them know that by allowing you to correct the issue, it prevents the issue from reoccurring. Advise your customer of how valuable their input is to the success of your business and even offer a token (discount on next purchase, free items, etc.) to express your gratitude.

Analyze the issue - Create a database of customer issues in order to identify negative business patterns. It's important to analyze your operations from your customer's viewpoint. The goal is to consistently provide great customer service. Your willingness to thoroughly examine why the issue happened and prevent it in the future is very important to maintaining a high rate of retention.

Remember, cherish the disgruntled customer. By voicing their dissatisfaction, they're giving you an opportunity to retain their business (and the business of others who might be impacted by the same issue) versus just silently allowing your competition an opportunity to replace you.

Exercise

1. How are you presently handling the disgruntled customer?

2. How often do leaders contact disgruntled customers for follow-up purposes?

3. What percentage of your disgruntled customers continues to utilize your products or services?

4. Is there a pattern in regards to why your customers are disgruntled?

Chapter 17 – Create a Customer Complaint System

My wife visited a major retail pharmacy with her mother to pick up medications. They arrived at the drive-through window about 30 minutes before closing and were immediately subjected to rude and abrupt behavior. Upon receiving the medications, her mother noticed that she did not need one of the medications provided. My wife pressed the drive through call button to advise the clerk of the need for a refund. After waiting for approximately 5 minutes for someone to respond, the clerk appeared and was advised of the need of a refund for the unneeded medication. Without verbally acknowledging the request, the clerk opened the drawer into which my wife placed the medication.

The wheels really started to come off of this customer service interaction as the clerk proceeded to slam the drawer shut. She returned and requested that my wife sign the refund receipt which was attached to a clipboard. After placing the clipboard with the attached signed receipt back into the drawer, the clerk slammed the drawer with such force that the clipboard was broken. My wife advised the clerk that she would be reported for her rude behavior. Promptly upon arriving home, my wife initiated an online complaint to the company and received a return email advising her that she would

91

receive an update within two business days. As promised, an update was received within the given timeframe apologizing for the clerk's behavior and advising that the customer relations department initiated an investigation of the complaint.

In the last chapter, we talked about the disgruntled customer. One of the tips given for handling this customer advised you to analyze the situation and create a database of customer complaints. This is important as it helps you to identify patterns in complaint types which will assist you in developing solid solutions. You might say, "Errol, I don't have time to put together something like this. Isn't it expensive to develop a complaint system?" Just as the company in the above story captured and responded to my wife's complaint, your ability to do the same is paramount to your success in delivering amazing customer service.

Developing a customer complaint system does not have to be neither time consuming or expensive. In being an analytical person by nature, I am always interested in gathering data in order to identify patterns. The first step in establishing this system is to determine what methods you will offer your customers to lodge complaints. Will you provide a complaint number to call? Will your customer be able to complain via your website through email or chat? What about text messaging? Don't forget that your customer can utilize social media to complain. Will you monitor that channel for complaints? The next step is to determine how you will compile your complaint information. My tool of choice is probably already loaded on your computer. It's called an Excel spreadsheet. This tool will work for those of you on a tight budget. Larger corporations have multiple software options for database creation. Choose which option works best for your situation. When building your complaint database, I suggest including the following:

Customer's Name/Account Number – You can sort your database by name to see if any your customers are having reoccurring or multiple issues.

Customer Gender – You can sort your database to see if certain complaints are gender oriented.

Complaint Date – This allows you to sort you database to determine when complaints are occurring.

Time Issue Occurred – Logging the issue occurrence time helps you to determine if certain issues are taking place at specific times.

Complaint - This is the complaint lodged by your customer.

Complaint code – Assign a code for the complaint type – for example – **2. Damaged Product When Received By Customer**. This allows you to sort your database by complaint type.

Complaint Area – Which area of your organization is responsible for the complaint? This allows you to sort your database by the department within your organization. (If applicable)

Complaint Source – This category allows you to see which method your customer utilizes to complain. (Phone, Face to Face, Email, Chat, Text)

These are some categories that I deem important. You can sort your database by several categories to get valuable information. For instance – you can sort your database to tell you how often a particular complaint (**Complaint code**) occurs, if it occurs more at a particular time (**Time of occurrence**) and is related to a specific area of your organization (**Complaint area**). This is just an example of the options available for analyzing data from your customer complaint database. It is crucial to determine if you have a complaint pattern developing within your organization as you may incur revenue losses along with a tarnished reputation if the complaints go unaddressed. Whatever method you utilize to track customer complaints, make sure you act upon your accumulated data. Data without follow-up actions are just dead numbers. Go above and beyond to personally contact the complaining customer to thank them for their complaint. Advise them of what was done to resolve the issue. Let the customer know how their complaint has assisted you in improving your operation. A complaint system is a critical component in your quest to deliver amazing customer service. Remember, a complaining customer is your best friend!

Exercise

1. How are customer complaints measured within your company?

2. How many customer complaints do your receive on a monthly basis?

3. Does a pattern exist in regards to the type of complaint?

4. What current plan is utilized to handle customer complaints?

5. Are you monitoring the social media channels for complaints about your company or your competitors?

Chapter 18 – Create A Customer Feedback System

In this chapter we'll talk about the importance of creating a customer feedback system. In the last chapter, we discussed the importance of creating a customer complaint system. There is one critical difference between the two. The customer feedback system is proactive in nature. You are reaching out to your customer to get their opinion in regards to your organization versus reacting to a customer complaint. Most people feel valued when asked "What do you think?" If you really are interested in delivering amazing customer service, then don't forget to ask your customers "What do you think?" What do you think about my product? What do you think about our service? Did we meet your expectations? How can we improve? How likely are you to buy our product/utilize our service again? How likely are you to refer others to us? All of these questions allow your customer to provide valuable feedback about your business. One way to gather this information is through customer service surveys.

Hold on before you say, "Errol, my business is much too small to survey our customers!" Allow me to share this story. My wife, Theresa, operates a virtual assistant business where she provides administrative support to small business owners. During the latter part of 2011, she was interested in determining how her customers felt about her service. I suggested she send out customer service surveys to get information regarding their satisfaction levels. The survey was created in Survey Monkey utilizing information Theresa gathers when meeting with a prospective customer. Her finished survey is what I call a two-tier survey. The first tier gathers responses to the customer's expectations regarding the virtual assistant industry:

It's important that my virtual assistant possess skills specific to my business requirements.

Disagree Somewhat Agree Agree   Strongly Agree

The second tier gets the customer to respond to Theresa's performance"

My assistant possesses skills specific to my business requirements.

Disagree Somewhat Agree Agree Strongly Agree

Should the customer state that he/she **Strongly Agrees** with the industry statement, anything less than **Strongly Agrees** when responding to the service provider's performance creates a gap that needs some attention. Customer service surveys can play a key role in the deliverance of great customer service as your customer's responses can identify opportunities for improvement. Your survey does not have to be complicated to be effective. I would suggest a 5 to 10 question survey.

As in the example above, think about what is important to the typical customer who chooses to utilize your product or service. If you're in the hospitality industry maybe a quick check-in process is important. On-line time is critical to customers of IT support providers. Ask your customers to rate your service in comparison to what's important to them. For the IT support firm that may mean asking the customer to rate how important on-line time is: It's important that our systems are online 99% of the time. Now let's find out how the IT support firm measures up by getting the customer to rate their performance in this area: XYZ Support keeps our systems online 99% of the time. If the customer states that they **Strongly Agree** that it's important that their systems are online 99% of the time, then XYZ Support better make sure that those systems are up 99% of the time!

Often I am asked "When is the best time to get feedback from my customer?" I always recommend getting feedback as soon as possible after interacting with your customer. If appropriate for your business, get feedback immediately after the purchase or interaction. The experience is still fresh in the customer's mind. Offer incentives to the customer for providing feedback – 10% off their next purchase, an opportunity to win a gift certificate or one of your company's products or services. When I visit my local office supply retailer, the check - out employees always make it a point to ask me to call the 1-800 # on the receipt to give my opinion regarding my store visit. Is this something you can incorporate into your business? Perhaps a small card with 5 survey questions will work for you. These two methods allow for immediate feedback regarding your service.

When you do not see your customer on a daily basis; such as in instances where your customer contracts with your business on a monthly basis; I suggest surveying your customer on a quarterly basis. Should your business utilize account managers, it's a good idea to solicit feedback from your customers on a monthly basis. I suggest making it a habit to attempt to get feedback during each customer interaction. Reassure your customers that it's okay for them to complain about your company or service. Make sure they understand how valuable their input is to the success of your company.

Another method for gathering feedback is through your customer contact employees. When your customer interacts with your employees, valuable information is available as a result. It's amazing what customers may say during these interactions – "I love this about your product or service, but I wish that you could...." Encourage your employees to share information regarding customer feedback and ideas on improving the customer experience. Develop methods for them to easily do so. Earlier in Chapter 17 we discussed the importance of creating a database to capture customer complaint information. Do the same for customer feedback information. If yours is a large corporation, make sure that your customer feedback databases are generic across the organization as this allows for easy data interpretation. You can accomplish this by developing a code system that's agreeable to all departments. Your customer's feedback will bring business blind spots to your attention. Soliciting information from your customer can prevent the need to respond to customer complaints. By proactively requesting feedback, you have an opportunity to improve your product or service before your customer makes the decision to complain. The decision to ask for feedback impacts your entire operation – 1. The need to respond to customer complaints is reduced as your customer is more than likely to give you an opportunity to improve their experience when you proactively solicit feedback. 2. Your customer retention rate is more apt to remain stable or even increase as a result. 3. Improved profitability is highly probable. Be consistent in soliciting feedback. Whatever frequency you chose, stick to it. By doing so, you're telling your customer that their opinion is important. Advise your customers of how their feedback has helped you to improve your products or services. Remember, customers like to know that their opinion is valued.

Exercise

1. What methods are you currently utilizing to gather customer feedback?

2. When do you solicit feedback from your customer?

3. How do you utilize the feedback information within your company?

4. What's the financial impact of utilizing your customer feedback?

Summary

Well there you have it. That's my viewpoint on what it takes to deliver great customer service. Hopefully my experiences can assist you in creating a customer centered culture as well as a great working environment. Just as balance is important in your personal life it's also important to balance your organization to meet both the needs of your customers and employees. These keys can open the doors of success whether yours is a small business or large corporation. It may seem as if doing so is a lot of work, but the end result is well worth the necessary labor to implement these keys. Each key alone can improve your business, but when all of the keys are utilized, a system is created. Your business will create loyal customers, loyal employees and new customers will appear because of what your present customers say you do for them. Close your eyes and think about what you would like your business to look like in the long run. Now open your eyes and get started! Remember to always treat others with respect, act with integrity, look to be of service, and have pride in your workmanship. These four principles form the framework for building a great organization. Hey, that sounds like the beginning of another book! Thanks for taking the time to read this book!

About The Author

Errol D. Allen

Errol Allen has over 25 years of hands – on experience in the customer service industry including 13 years in a management role. Errol has worked in several industries within the service sector including security systems, newspaper, software, cable television and insurance. Having held positions as an Internal Customer Service Consultant, Call Center Quality Manager and Operations Analyst, Errol understands that a "systems" orientation is crucial to providing excellent customer service. He is experienced in facilitating interdepartmental process improvement projects to insure efficient service delivery to both internal and external customers. Errol has also designed and implemented customer service training programs for the "front line" associate to insure employee confidence when interacting with customers. He is a member of the American Society of Quality, which promotes the practical application of quality knowledge across multiple industries. Errol shares his customer service expertise as a contributing writer for **Small Business Today Magazine** and **D-Mars Business Journal** and is the publisher of **"Now That's Customer Service!"**, a free online monthly newsletter where he offers customer service tips and real life customer service stories. In his quest to acknowledge the receipt of great customer service, Errol personally awards his **"Now That's Customer Service!** award to deserving employees or companies. An avid blogger, his articles have been published in several online magazines including **Customer Service Manager** and **Customer Experience Magazine** of the **UK**. He is also a workshop leader at the **University of Houston's Small Business Development Center.** Errol resides in Houston, Texas with his wife Theresa.

Need A Speaker?

Errol is a public speaker with topics such as:

Loyalty – A Two Street

Customer Loyalty & Satisfaction

Why Smile Training Alone Is Not Enough

Need Assistance With Your Customer Service?

Errol seeks to help his consulting clients develop customer service strategies for maximum customer retention. Visit Errol's website at www.errolallenconsulting.com to learn more about the services offered by Errol Allen Consulting and subscribe to **"Now That's Customer Service!"**, Errol's free monthly online newsletter. Email Errol at errol@errolallenconsulting.com.

9547383R00076

Printed in Great Britain
by Amazon.co.uk, Ltd.,
Marston Gate.